ON A WINDLESS NIGHT

Natalli M. Amato

Ra Press
100 Kennedy Drive #53
South Burlington, VT 05403

For My Mother

ISBN 978-0-359-83707-6

"Whoever you are, no matter how lonely,
the world offers itself to your imagination,
calls to you like the wild geese, harsh and exciting -
over and over announcing your place
in the family of things."

- Mary Oliver

Introduction:

I'm ten years old, standing in a gaggle of neighbors and cousins, playing four-square in the middle of the road. There are no cars to worry about. Everyone we know is already here: vehicles parked in the driveway and bodies parked in lawn chairs. Most of us wear this year's edition of Old Navy's Fourth of July t-shirt. Some of us wear sunscreen. Others forgot. Some sport skinned knees. Other's wear the day's tumbles on knobby elbows. We all have lake water in our hair.

Every porch has a barefoot mother or grandmother using all of her lungpower to announce it's dinner time. There's a shared understanding between Morgia's Beach kids that whatever meals we are matched with will be scarfed down with speed so we can meet back by The Big Tree. Our landmarks are not recorded on maps, yet they are unquestionably important - to us.

Summers pass. Four-square turns to night swims and bonfires. The Big Tree is too close to our parents for it to still be our spot. There's a thirty rack hidden in the brush by the Second Speed Bump. We fill the night with country songs that both celebrate the beauty of small towns like ours and plant the idea that someday, we may have to leave. Actually picturing that far-off day is impossible when we can hardly contemplate the coming of fall.

I would easily believe that these changes occurred overnight, perhaps when we were distracted by the fireworks overhead. Yet, there is a box under my bed of journals stating that this cannot be true, as if the young girl who wrote them marked down the dates only because she knew she'd be called upon to prove them to a skeptic.

These poems begin there. While many were conjured in Syracuse University classrooms where two poets (Sarah Harwell, Brooks Haxton) treated me as if I were one, too, these images and feelings were germinating long before I discovered poets aren't confined to the past; they're walking and talking and breathing and writing right here in Upstate New York.

For those who also define home as Lake Ontario (Sackets Harbor to be precise, Morgia's Beach to be exact), these poems will be familiar even when reading them for the very first time because our memories are entangled in the same geography. I hope these readers will regard the words I've chosen in an attempt to pin this place to the page as truthful.

Those, however, who don't know the young girl with her journal, who haven't shared my Sunday dinner table or four square chalk, who know this region as only a place to visit and not the setting of their own story - I hope you find it deserving of a dot on your map or maybe even something more: a red pushpin saying, "Here. Here is something small, but important."

Natalli Amato

Lake Ontario Afternoon

Perched on the splintered dock's edge,
two pairs of toes wriggle like worms in mid-air,
too short to disrupt the cotton clouds mirrored in the water.
A rusting fishing boat bobs with the breeze,
sun-dried seaweed's fishy musk crinkles the freshly freckled noses,
pollywogs dart, a skittish dance, away from a winged shadow,
two strawberry blonde ponytails turn toward Grandmother, yelling, *supper!*

The Milkweed

Past the rusting gate without the lock,
just before the picnic table
lined with freshly picked tomatoes
and a mason jar filled with worn-soft ones,
a pink bicycle pauses on the right-hand side,
training wheels lodged in the space between gravel chunks.

The milkweed's tear-shaped pods swell, plump.
Tufts of wispy white seed escape on the breeze.
A monarch caterpillar rests on an oval leaf,
his orange stripe thicker than his black bookends.
Curious hands pluck the leaf.
Silky, sticky whiteness seeps into the palm's crevices.

Childhood's Vocabulary List

Helicopter seeds. Seagull soup. Goop.
Fairy dust. Wishing Rock. Stuck in muck.
Bloodsucker. Big ol' snapper.
Lightning bug. Mother Goose. Coydog loose.
Camp jammies. Hear the croakies.

Sprinkler

Under the cottonwood tree
where seed floats on the offshore breeze
I see us, still children,
running through the garden hose spray
shrieking from a simple joy
the chill of clear water
landing on tender skin.

Walking To the Treehouse

Deep enough into the woods
for us to imagine a new game, and play it,
the ATV tracks we've trailed give way to tall grass.

There are no treetops to obstruct the clouds,
dense like lamb's fleece.

Grandfather tells us there are ticks in these parts.
Still, we bear our bony, skinned knees.

Thimbleberries grow along the clearing's edge.
We brought no basket, only bellies,
to collect the red morsels
plucked from the dried stars that bore them,
placed between giggling lips.

When I Am Shucking Corn

I am shucking corn for Sunday supper,
strands of silk fall to my toes.
Grandfather's liver-spotted hands
work faster than mine,
he lets me know it.

We look out across the lake,
the September sun lowers itself
to the horizon.
I pause my work, unlike Grandfather,
until the sun is nearly invisible.

I wish it were higher in the sky.

My Mother Never Taught Me How to Clean

After pressing wildflowers between old encyclopedias,
after helping the peapod plant's tendrils grasp the chicken wire,
after gathering smooth rocks for worry stones,
Clean up fell last on your list of instructions, only after
Go read a book
Be gentle
Look at that butterfly
Call your grandmother
Write me a story
until supper
where we set the table for two, two plates next to hodgepodge piles
of bills, photos, dog-eared magazines, recipes you thought you'd try
instead of the overcooked chicken, which I still scarf down
as long as you let me leave the radio on loud-
Garth Brooks, Reba, George Strait, our dinner party guests.
When it's time for dessert, my small frame tries to fill the passenger seat
and you open the sunroof even though the wind teases your hair.
My toes leave a family of circular smudges on the windshield and
when we pull up to the ice cream stand, neither of us thinks twice about
our bare feet on asphalt.
More sprinkles find a place on my shirt than in my mouth
but before you reach for napkins, you point across the road, *look!*
Look at the sunset.

43°55N/76°7W

You knew me in a pickup truck before
the rust got to the frame
and it was sent to the junkyard
to become a forgotten thing -
when the back roads were still gravel
and our grandfathers insisted
on filling in the potholes themselves.

I knew you as the master of the screen-door sneak-out
before your mother replaced *cottage*
with *lakehouse* -
when the squeaky doors and chipping tiles could be ignored
for one more summer.

We knew each other in a space in time
where we picked off our innocence,
that blistering, itching scab.

Winter Sunrise

We do not speak
though,
      Once,
         we did.

I do not speak to caterpillars,
fairies, ladybugs in mason jars,
though,
      Once,
         I did.

Sitting in the open hatchback of your parents' car
we staved off March's chill with a thermos of cocoa
waiting for sunrise to thaw the frozen lake from its imposed stillness.

While my eyes hung heavy from interrupted slumber,
you looked out at barren ice and saw trapped moonlight,
paused moments, the lake in her bridal gown.
Then,
    you
       showed me.

An August Night in the North Country

Bullfrogs belt their baritone blues.
Crickets chirp in continuous cadence.
Cattails lightly brush the tallgrass, murmuring indecipherable verse.
Intertwined treetops part over the pathway below
Where I stumble over stones, my neck craned to glimpse Orion.

Meteor Shower

Tonight the newsman called for lustrous lights more magnificent
than the stars I already adore.
From my blanket spread out on the front lawn,
the only lights I see are the orange reflectors
on Mr. Tirinato's fishing boat,
the blue glow of the Sboro's living room TV,
the dim yellow hue from the new lamppost
that the village recently voted to install.
Perhaps tonight I will marvel at the ordinary,
at my neighbors, whose existence is so near to mine
and the tiny flickers of brightness we humbly present to the world.
Suppose Halley told her comets
tonight down below there would be fireflies and bonfires,
homebound headlights and neon rest stop signs,
front porches left aglow and welcome home kisses.
Perhaps they are peering behind the clouds,
marveling.

Closing Up the Brew Pub

A black Old Navy tee shirt hides crusty ketchup, pickle juice,
Fryer grease, spilled Mountain Dew, twelve hours of sweating
through a double shift, Labor Day Weekend.
Danielle flips barstools on their heads and volunteers to take the trash,
A cigarette protruding from her dyed-black hair, tucked behind her ear.
Someone's kid sister doodles hearts in the reservation book,
Unwilling to mop until she's given her to-go box of wings.
Busboys sneak PBRs from the refrigerator, cargo pant pockets bulging.
Pearl sits across from me, making square napkins triangular.
I take from her growing pile, swaddling each around a knife and fork,
Left corner, fold, right corner, fold, roll, repeat.
From our booth, we hear the kitchen radio blaring
Bonnie Raitt and with a softness seldom used on the clock,
We sing to ourselves while Gail runs the vacuum.

To believe in this living is just a hard way to go

This is not a death poem

because those do not have fireworks,
Jello-shots,
Hoffman hot dogs on a charcoal grill,
puckered pink sunburns,
the sweet scent of gasoline on an open lake,
children shouting *again! again!* from an intertube,
waterproof speakers blasting Pearl Jam on top of a Yeti cooler.

This is not a death poem because
the forest grew by taking in your exhales,
the mountains echoed your laughter so often that birds learned to sing,
and nobody opens a can of Miller Lite without telling the story of you,
still in the present tense.

Opening the Cottage

Paint is peeling from the porch's planks.
A ladybug sized hole gapes in the screen door.
Windows whine after a year unopened.
Sunflower seed shaped droppings litter the insides of kitchen cabinets.
With Spring comes muddied work boots, elbow-length rubber gloves,
the quiet tinkering with worn furniture.

I pause when washing the window to watch the Robin -
her small beak grips a dried flower stalk from last year's garden
as she hops through the overgrown grass
toward the tree that will soon hold her nest.

Camp Library

Untouched, the books
lose their color to the sun
casting its light through the window.
Farmer's Almanac, Adirondack
field guides, watercolor sketches
of irritant plants.

The books collect your fingerprints no longer,
only dust of dissipated cobwebs.
Who will be the first to break this isolation?
Too soon, so soon.

One day, once more, much later,
we will spy majesty
in a black bear. You
will lead us back
to the shelf of all you knew
yet did not get to teach.

Light Travels

I.

In hushed reverence
reserved for folklore
you speak
of light years, life
spans, finite speed,
Distance -
measured.

This is the hour
droplets attach
to long grass,
feet are wet
with what will be
morning's dew.

There, you tell me
seeing the stars is
seeing the past.

II.

Oh, how far the light has come
to touch me.
Will I see you,
always?

The Dandelion

When I was no longer looking
yellow florets grayed, leaving
a porous bauble in place

and just like all beauty
I failed to recognize in time,
it dispersed with no more than a child's breath -
slowly, gliding away.

Hiding From the Dinner Rush

Heavy metal screams through the holes in the screen door.
From the sagging back steps,
I hear cooks curse at the onslaught of yellow tickets.
There are credit cards to run, drafts to pour,
cheesecakes to retrieve from the walk-in freezer.
Yet here I sit, picking at the splintering wood,
brittle as the mascara overstaying its welcome on my lashes.
Mosquitoes land on my legs, slick with sweat and spilled vinegar.
I look out at the harbor, where darkness ushers boats back to the marina.
A sailboat slices the sunset's reflection with the smoothness of its hull.
The same breeze filling its sail touches my face.
I yearn for its ease, then, return inside.

Winter in the Cabin

Brittle needles fall
from pines lining the property,
landing atop powder snowfall,
then buried.

Supper simmers on the stove. I look
for your truck in the drive,
an old instinct.

Fire crackles in the woodstove.
Dryness leaves my lips chapped,
cracked. There was always
balm in your pocket.

As I cross the room,
wool socks separate
my feet from knotted floorboards
we laid with our own hands.

I reach for the evergreen flannel
that fit your shoulders
before mine. I
feel the draft,
still.

The Cornfield

The last time we were here there was no sun
to cast the promised hue across the pasture.
There were no swaying stems for the breeze to comb,
only wilted, brittle spindles bent down into the earth.
Even the deepest roots could not reach ground that remained unfrozen,
and our walk once paced with chatter turned wordless.
But watch how the farmer has returned to till the soil.
Watch him spread manure and resist plugging your nose.
This too is fresh air.
This too is a scent we could miss.
Watch how the farmer cares for the land that has taken from him.
Watch him believe it will give again.

Stopping in Glenwood Cemetery

The mallard etched into my father's headstone
unnerves me. Was it not dipping its emerald
head beneath the pond's surface moments ago?
The grass is littered -
a cork separated from its whiskey,
stray shells missing from a shotgun.

The engine of my truck rumbles, idle, behind me
while I thumb these remainders -
wondering what it would have been like
to know him well enough
to bring more than just my body,
still pumping his blood.

The Flood

Carp swim in the front lawn
where, just yesterday, we danced
barefoot through the sprinklers, risking clover.
But these waves are not the easy ripples of yesterday-
They arch upwards, crash with force.
In the swamp, the great tree has been uprooted.
It won't be long before the pooling water
reaches the porch and the lake reclaims land
we only thought was ours.

On A Windless Night

lunar light licks the lake's surface
to near stillness.
Somewhere
in the vastness,
water meets sky.
Here, from my lawn chair
in the darkened yard,
I cannot see such a place.
Night is seamless
and I hope it takes me
as it has the moon
which hangs in suspension,
touching nothing.
Reaching everything.

He Finds Me On the Trail

From the long grass on the roadside
an old friend beckons me to pause
for an overdue hello. Our language, now,
is the wordless one of the wild.
Against fine goldthread petals and
dame's rocket, purple exuberance,
his crimson belly protrudes
perched on a twig,
the stop sign of the forest. Stop I do
to touch this strewn bouquet
with my nose
for a whiff of fragrance, reassurance,
before he remembers the mortal in me
and must, quickly, fly away.

Root Vegetable Soup

Worthy of regal invitations, Mother's cursive knew only recipe cards:
One large onion, parsnips, rutabaga, peeled and cut.
One inky, swooping star sharing the same line as lemon juice.
Her kitchen window frames generations of Sunday afternoon football throwers,
book review connoisseurs. I glance up from her cutting board, wave,
while conversation and wafts of garlic pass through the window screen.
From her chair, an old wedding gift, she practices a new lesson-
Patience, humming lightly
in place of suggesting I not forget to add the lemon.

Leaving Navy Point

We step off the boat wearing new freckles.
Sunset tonight comes with a coolness and
my newly browned skin draws from its reserve of sunshine.
I cannot see over the cooler I carry, topped with towels,
but my toes know the planks of the floating dock
leading me to grass.
Amidst the low rush of reaching waves,
I hear metallic snaps as you fit the cover on the vessel
while I pack our afternoon into the truck bed.
Low in the orange sky,
the moon hangs between sailing masts.
Our swimsuits transfer dampness
to the cloth seats. No need to fuss
over a truck on its second generation.
The radio comes in well.
There is time for one or two Eagles songs
before we make the left turn home.

The Farmhouse Kitchen

Beyond the garden, the faint yellow of sunrise
brightens the pasture. I crouch
on the stone step path
pushing aside overgrown weeds, dill,
yellow mustard flowers,
in favor of rosemary.
Dull scissors leave the stalks frayed, uneven.
Sprigs settle in my lap.
I glance up from my task
to find a goat supervising through the fence beams.
His eyes, the color of the earth beneath my feet, hold my gaze -
not unlike the grey-haired man
who also knew how much work one day could hold
when he called for rains and poured my coffee
in this morning's lightless hour.

Waking On a Sunday

Warbling chirps fill the spaces between the tree's leaves.
A lawnmower's engine amplifies when it nears the window.
The neighbor's conversation reaches through the screen.

Me, I'm late to join the day.
The tickle of a breeze sent forth by the lake
keeps me drifting between here and the elsewhere of dreams.

Remembering Thompson Park

The sky resembles the pink peonies
spilling over in the garden.

Every proclamation of wonder
I've uttered in this world
is true, again.

Lavender stalls the darkness
and I must tell you, now,
that I have not forgotten
our conversation on the hill
where we had to crack the windows
to let a few dreams out.
The car was brimming, full.

August in the Garden

Black-eyed Susans leave no space unoccupied
between fair daisies, fuchsia cosmos.

Snapped, scrapped stalks were unguarded by the Marigolds.
Rabbits are much bolder this summer, it appears.

Sunflowers grow taller than the cottage roof
hiding missing shingles from sight.

There are weeds but I don't much care to pull them.
Look! The Monarch visits anyways.

Stargazing
for Jamie R.

Strapped under a plastic helmet are
eyes, shaped like mine, and
a nose shared by her father's family.
Features peek out from a mop of wavy hair
granted by neither side, only lake water.

I skinned my knee on this same road,
hid the blood so Mother would not pull me inside,
loved how the fishy wind dried my flesh,
infused me with itself.

Watching her wobble on wheels, I only remember the sting.
So I pull weeds from the garden
to remind my saner self that a little dirt is good for a person.
Across the lawn,
small feet on small pedals learn they are capable of speed. There,
I see the stars.

Frog Catching

Each time I discover a true thing about myself
it becomes a frog leaping from my cupped hands
returning to the reeds having learned what a net is
and how to avoid one.

Then there is the girl not yet taller than the cattails
traipsing between swamp and forest
swinging her butterfly net through the air
happily catching nothing.

Author's Note:

Certain poems in this collection simply would not exist without words from voices other than my own.

The final line of "Closing Up the Brewpub" was borrowed from "Angel from Montgomery," penned by John Prine.

Standing in the front lawn, watching her kids ride bikes, Jamie Rabideau said, "it's like seeing the stars." She can make plain, barefoot, neighborly conversation poetic. I attempted to do her justice with "Stargazing."

ABOUT THE AUTHOR:

Natalli Amato is the Assistant to the Editor for *Rolling Stone.*

During her time as an undergraduate at Syracuse University, she was awarded the 2019 Edwin T. Whiffen Poetry Prize for her poem, *"When I Am Shucking Corn."*

The previous year, she was a runner up for the same prize, as well as the Stephen Crane Fiction Prize.

She is from Sackets Harbor, New York.

CPSIA information can be obtained
at www.ICGtesting.com
Printed in the USA
BVHW030014051019
560246BV00002B/255/P

9 780359 837076